This garden planner belongs to

CW00954420

_____

_____

Thank you for your purchase

wich made us very happy. We hope we did the same for you with this log book. Please leave us an honest review on Amazon if you have the pleasure. You should know that our business thrives because of people like you

Feel free to write to us if you wish at publinext@yahoo.com

Name _____

Location _____

Supplier _____

Price _____

Name

GERMINATED	
PLANTED	
HARVESTED	

Started From

○ SEED   ○ PLANT

Light Level

○ SUN   ○ PARTIAL SUN   ○ SHADE   ○ OTHER

Scientific Class

○ VEGETABLE   ○ FRUIT   ○ HERB   ○ FLOWER   ○ SHRUB   ○ TREE
○ ANNUAL   ○ BIENNIAL   ○ PERENNIAL   ○ SEEDLING

Care Instructions

Planting Instructions

Additional Notes

Fertilizer & Equipment

Fertilizer & Equipment

SIZE	☆☆☆☆☆
COLOR	☆☆☆☆☆
TASTE	☆☆☆☆☆

Name _____

Location _____

Supplier _____

Price _____

Name

| GERMINATED |
| PLANTED |
| HARVESTED |

Started From

○ SEED   ○ PLANT

Light Level

○ SUN   ○ PARTIAL SUN   ○ SHADE   ○ OTHER

Scientific Class

○ VEGETABLE   ○ FRUIT   ○ HERB   ○ FLOWER   ○ SHRUB   ○ TREE
○ ANNUAL   ○ BIENNIAL   ○ PERENNIAL   ○ SEEDLING

Care Instructions

Planting Instructions

Additional Notes

Fertilizer & Equipment

Fertilizer & Equipment

SIZE	☆☆☆☆☆
COLOR	☆☆☆☆☆
TASTE	☆☆☆☆☆

Name _____

Location _____

Supplier _____

Price _____

Name

GERMINATED	
PLANTED	
HARVESTED	

Started From

○ SEED ○ PLANT

Light Level

○ SUN ○ PARTIAL SUN ○ SHADE ○ OTHER

Scientific Class

○ VEGETABLE ○ FRUIT ○ HERB ○ FLOWER ○ SHRUB ○ TREE
○ ANNUAL ○ BIENNIAL ○ PERENNIAL ○ SEEDLING

Care Instructions

Planting Instructions

Additional Notes

Fertilizer & Equipment

Fertilizer & Equipment

SIZE	☆☆☆☆☆
COLOR	☆☆☆☆☆
TASTE	☆☆☆☆☆

Name _____

Location _____

Supplier _____

Price _____

Name

GERMINATED	
PLANTED	
HARVESTED	

Started From

- ◯ SEED
- ◯ PLANT

Light Level

- ◯ SUN
- ◯ PARTIAL SUN
- ◯ SHADE
- ◯ OTHER

Scientific Class

- ◯ VEGETABLE
- ◯ FRUIT
- ◯ HERB
- ◯ FLOWER
- ◯ SHRUB
- ◯ TREE
- ◯ ANNUAL
- ◯ BIENNIAL
- ◯ PERENNIAL
- ◯ SEEDLING

Care Instructions

Planting Instructions

Additional Notes

Fertilizer & Equipment

Fertilizer & Equipment

SIZE	☆☆☆☆☆
COLOR	☆☆☆☆☆
TASTE	☆☆☆☆☆

Name _____

Location _____

Supplier _____

Price _____

Name

GERMINATED	
PLANTED	
HARVESTED	

Started From

○ SEED   ○ PLANT

Light Level

○ SUN   ○ PARTIAL SUN   ○ SHADE   ○ OTHER

Scientific Class

○ VEGETABLE   ○ FRUIT   ○ HERB   ○ FLOWER   ○ SHRUB   ○ TREE
○ ANNUAL   ○ BIENNIAL   ○ PERENNIAL   ○ SEEDLING

Care Instructions

Planting Instructions

Additional Notes

Fertilizer & Equipment

Fertilizer & Equipment

SIZE	☆☆☆☆☆
COLOR	☆☆☆☆☆
TASTE	☆☆☆☆☆

Name _____

Location _____

Supplier _____

Price _____

Name

GERMINATED	
PLANTED	
HARVESTED	

Started From

○ SEED   ○ PLANT

Light Level

○ SUN   ○ PARTIAL SUN   ○ SHADE   ○ OTHER

Scientific Class

○ VEGETABLE   ○ FRUIT   ○ HERB   ○ FLOWER   ○ SHRUB   ○ TREE
○ ANNUAL   ○ BIENNIAL   ○ PERENNIAL   ○ SEEDLING

Care Instructions

Planting Instructions

Additional Notes

Fertilizer & Equipment

Fertilizer & Equipment

SIZE	☆☆☆☆☆
COLOR	☆☆☆☆☆
TASTE	☆☆☆☆☆

Name _____

Location _____

Supplier _____

Price _____

Name

GERMINATED	
PLANTED	
HARVESTED	

Started From

○ SEED   ○ PLANT   ○ SUN   ○ PARTIAL SUN   ○ SHADE   ○ OTHER

Light Level

Scientific Class

○ VEGETABLE   ○ FRUIT   ○ HERB   ○ FLOWER   ○ SHRUB   ○ TREE
○ ANNUAL   ○ BIENNIAL   ○ PERENNIAL   ○ SEEDLING

Care Instructions

Planting Instructions

Additional Notes

Fertilizer & Equipment

Fertilizer & Equipment

SIZE	☆☆☆☆☆
COLOR	☆☆☆☆☆
TASTE	☆☆☆☆☆

Name _____

Name

GERMINATED	
PLANTED	
HARVESTED	

Location _____

Supplier _____

Price _____

Started From

○ SEED   ○ PLANT

Light Level

○ SUN   ○ PARTIAL SUN   ○ SHADE   ○ OTHER

Scientific Class

○ VEGETABLE   ○ FRUIT   ○ HERB   ○ FLOWER   ○ SHRUB   ○ TREE

○ ANNUAL   ○ BIENNIAL   ○ PERENNIAL   ○ SEEDLING

Care Instructions

Planting Instructions

Additional Notes

Fertilizer & Equipment

Fertilizer & Equipment

SIZE	☆☆☆☆☆
COLOR	☆☆☆☆☆
TASTE	☆☆☆☆☆

Name _____

Location _____

Supplier _____

Price _____

Name

GERMINATED	
PLANTED	
HARVESTED	

Started From

○ SEED ○ PLANT

Light Level

○ SUN ○ PARTIAL SUN ○ SHADE ○ OTHER

Scientific Class

○ VEGETABLE ○ FRUIT ○ HERB ○ FLOWER ○ SHRUB ○ TREE

○ ANNUAL ○ BIENNIAL ○ PERENNIAL ○ SEEDLING

Care Instructions

Planting Instructions

Additional Notes

Fertilizer & Equipment

Fertilizer & Equipment

SIZE	☆☆☆☆☆
COLOR	☆☆☆☆☆
TASTE	☆☆☆☆☆

Name _____

Name

Location _____

GERMINATED	
PLANTED	
HARVESTED	

Supplier _____

Price _____

Started From

Light Level

( ) SEED   ( ) PLANT   ( ) SUN   ( ) PARTIAL SUN   ( ) SHADE   ( ) OTHER

Scientific Class

( ) VEGETABLE   ( ) FRUIT   ( ) HERB   ( ) FLOWER   ( ) SHRUB   ( ) TREE

( ) ANNUAL   ( ) BIENNIAL   ( ) PERENNIAL ( ) SEEDLING

Care Instructions

Planting Instructions

Additional Notes

Fertilizer & Equipment

Fertilizer & Equipment

SIZE	☆☆☆☆☆
COLOR	☆☆☆☆☆
TASTE	☆☆☆☆☆

Name _____

Location _____

Supplier _____

Price _____

GERMINATED	
PLANTED	
HARVESTED	

Started From

○ SEED ○ PLANT

Light Level

○ SUN ○ PARTIAL SUN ○ SHADE ○ OTHER

Scientific Class

○ VEGETABLE ○ FRUIT ○ HERB ○ FLOWER ○ SHRUB ○ TREE
○ ANNUAL ○ BIENNIAL ○ PERENNIAL ○ SEEDLING

Care Instructions

Planting Instructions

Additional Notes

Fertilizer & Equipment

Fertilizer & Equipment

SIZE	☆☆☆☆☆
COLOR	☆☆☆☆☆
TASTE	☆☆☆☆☆

Name _____

Location _____

Supplier _____

Price _____

Name

| GERMINATED |
| PLANTED |
| HARVESTED |

Started From

Light Level

○ SEED   ○ PLANT   ○ SUN   ○ PARTIAL SUN   ○ SHADE   ○ OTHER

Scientific Class

○ VEGETABLE   ○ FRUIT   ○ HERB   ○ FLOWER   ○ SHRUB   ○ TREE
○ ANNUAL   ○ BIENNIAL   ○ PERENNIAL   ○ SEEDLING

Care Instructions

Planting Instructions

Additional Notes

Fertilizer & Equipment

Fertilizer & Equipment

SIZE	☆☆☆☆☆
COLOR	☆☆☆☆☆
TASTE	☆☆☆☆☆

Name _____

Location _____

Supplier _____

Price _____

Name

| GERMINATED |
| PLANTED |
| HARVESTED |

Started From

○ SEED ○ PLANT

Light Level

○ SUN ○ PARTIAL SUN ○ SHADE ○ OTHER

Scientific Class

○ VEGETABLE ○ FRUIT ○ HERB ○ FLOWER ○ SHRUB ○ TREE
○ ANNUAL ○ BIENNIAL ○ PERENNIAL ○ SEEDLING

Care Instructions

Planting Instructions

Additional Notes

Fertilizer & Equipment

Fertilizer & Equipment

SIZE	☆☆☆☆☆
COLOR	☆☆☆☆☆
TASTE	☆☆☆☆☆

Name _____

Location _____

Supplier _____

Price _____

Name

GERMINATED
PLANTED
HARVESTED

Started From

○ SEED   ○ PLANT   ○ SUN   ○ PARTIAL SUN   ○ SHADE   ○ OTHER

Light Level

Scientific Class

○ VEGETABLE   ○ FRUIT   ○ HERB   ○ FLOWER   ○ SHRUB   ○ TREE
○ ANNUAL   ○ BIENNIAL   ○ PERENNIAL   ○ SEEDLING

Care Instructions

Planting Instructions

Additional Notes

Fertilizer & Equipment

Fertilizer & Equipment

SIZE	☆☆☆☆☆
COLOR	☆☆☆☆☆
TASTE	☆☆☆☆☆

Name _____

Location _____

Supplier _____

Price _____

Name

GERMINATED	
PLANTED	
HARVESTED	

Started From

| ○ SEED | ○ PLANT |

Light Level

| ○ SUN | ○ PARTIAL SUN | ○ SHADE | ○ OTHER |

Scientific Class

| ○ VEGETABLE | ○ FRUIT | ○ HERB | ○ FLOWER | ○ SHRUB | ○ TREE |
| ○ ANNUAL | ○ BIENNIAL | ○ PERENNIAL | ○ SEEDLING | | |

Care Instructions

Planting Instructions

Additional Notes

Fertilizer & Equipment

Fertilizer & Equipment

SIZE	☆☆☆☆☆
COLOR	☆☆☆☆☆
TASTE	☆☆☆☆☆

Name _____

Location _____

Supplier _____

Price _____

Name

GERMINATED
PLANTED
HARVESTED

Started From

○ SEED	○ PLANT

Light Level

○ SUN	○ PARTIAL SUN	○ SHADE	○ OTHER

Scientific Class

○ VEGETABLE	○ FRUIT	○ HERB	○ FLOWER	○ SHRUB	○ TREE
○ ANNUAL	○ BIENNIAL	○ PERENNIAL	○ SEEDLING		

Care Instructions

Planting Instructions

Additional Notes

Fertilizer & Equipment

Fertilizer & Equipment

SIZE	☆☆☆☆☆
COLOR	☆☆☆☆☆
TASTE	☆☆☆☆☆

Name _____

Location _____

Supplier _____

Price _____

Name

GERMINATED	
PLANTED	
HARVESTED	

Started From

Light Level

○ SEED ○ PLANT ○ SUN ○ PARTIAL SUN ○ SHADE ○ OTHER

Scientific Class

○ VEGETABLE ○ FRUIT ○ HERB ○ FLOWER ○ SHRUB ○ TREE
○ ANNUAL ○ BIENNIAL ○ PERENNIAL ○ SEEDLING

Care Instructions

Planting Instructions

Additional Notes

Fertilizer & Equipment

Fertilizer & Equipment

SIZE	☆☆☆☆☆
COLOR	☆☆☆☆☆
TASTE	☆☆☆☆☆

Name _____

Location _____

Supplier _____

Price _____

Name

| GERMINATED |
| PLANTED |
| HARVESTED |

Started From

○ SEED ○ PLANT ○ SUN ○ PARTIAL SUN ○ SHADE ○ OTHER

Light Level

Scientific Class

○ VEGETABLE ○ FRUIT ○ HERB ○ FLOWER ○ SHRUB ○ TREE
○ ANNUAL ○ BIENNIAL ○ PERENNIAL ○ SEEDLING

Care Instructions

Planting Instructions

Additional Notes

Fertilizer & Equipment

Fertilizer & Equipment

SIZE	☆☆☆☆☆
COLOR	☆☆☆☆☆
TASTE	☆☆☆☆☆

Name _____

Location _____

Supplier _____

Price _____

Name

GERMINATED	
PLANTED	
HARVESTED	

Started From

○ SEED   ○ PLANT

Light Level

○ SUN   ○ PARTIAL SUN   ○ SHADE   ○ OTHER

Scientific Class

○ VEGETABLE   ○ FRUIT   ○ HERB   ○ FLOWER   ○ SHRUB   ○ TREE
○ ANNUAL   ○ BIENNIAL   ○ PERENNIAL   ○ SEEDLING

Care Instructions

Planting Instructions

Additional Notes

Fertilizer & Equipment

Fertilizer & Equipment

SIZE	☆☆☆☆☆
COLOR	☆☆☆☆☆
TASTE	☆☆☆☆☆

Name _____

Location _____

Supplier _____

Price _____

Name

GERMINATED	
PLANTED	
HARVESTED	

Started From

○ SEED   ○ PLANT

Light Level

○ SUN   ○ PARTIAL SUN   ○ SHADE   ○ OTHER

Scientific Class

○ VEGETABLE   ○ FRUIT   ○ HERB   ○ FLOWER   ○ SHRUB   ○ TREE
○ ANNUAL   ○ BIENNIAL   ○ PERENNIAL   ○ SEEDLING

Care Instructions

Planting Instructions

Additional Notes

Fertilizer & Equipment

Fertilizer & Equipment

SIZE	☆☆☆☆☆
COLOR	☆☆☆☆☆
TASTE	☆☆☆☆☆

Name _____

Location _____

Supplier _____

Price _____

Name

GERMINATED	
PLANTED	
HARVESTED	

Started From

| ○ SEED | ○ PLANT | ○ SUN | ○ PARTIAL SUN | ○ SHADE | ○ OTHER |

Light Level

Scientific Class

| ○ VEGETABLE | ○ FRUIT | ○ HERB | ○ FLOWER | ○ SHRUB | ○ TREE |
| ○ ANNUAL | ○ BIENNIAL | ○ PERENNIAL | ○ SEEDLING | | |

Care Instructions

Planting Instructions

Additional Notes

Fertilizer & Equipment

Fertilizer & Equipment

SIZE	☆☆☆☆☆
COLOR	☆☆☆☆☆
TASTE	☆☆☆☆☆

Name _____

Name

Location _____

| GERMINATED |
| PLANTED |
| HARVESTED |

Supplier _____

Price _____

Started From

○ SEED	○ PLANT

Light Level

○ SUN	○ PARTIAL SUN	○ SHADE	○ OTHER

Scientific Class

○ VEGETABLE	○ FRUIT	○ HERB	○ FLOWER	○ SHRUB	○ TREE
○ ANNUAL	○ BIENNIAL	○ PERENNIAL	○ SEEDLING		

Care Instructions

Planting Instructions

Additional Notes

Fertilizer & Equipment

Fertilizer & Equipment

SIZE	☆☆☆☆☆
COLOR	☆☆☆☆☆
TASTE	☆☆☆☆☆

Name _____

Location _____

Supplier _____

Price _____

Name

GERMINATED	
PLANTED	
HARVESTED	

Started From

( ) SEED   ( ) PLANT   ( ) SUN   ( ) PARTIAL SUN   ( ) SHADE   ( ) OTHER

Light Level

Scientific Class

( ) VEGETABLE   ( ) FRUIT   ( ) HERB   ( ) FLOWER   ( ) SHRUB   ( ) TREE

( ) ANNUAL   ( ) BIENNIAL   ( ) PERENNIAL   ( ) SEEDLING

Care Instructions

Planting Instructions

Additional Notes

Fertilizer & Equipment

Fertilizer & Equipment

SIZE	☆☆☆☆☆
COLOR	☆☆☆☆☆
TASTE	☆☆☆☆☆

Name _____

Location _____

Supplier _____

Price _____

Name

| GERMINATED |
| PLANTED |
| HARVESTED |

Started From

| ○ SEED | ○ PLANT |

Light Level

| ○ SUN | ○ PARTIAL SUN | ○ SHADE | ○ OTHER |

Scientific Class

| ○ VEGETABLE | ○ FRUIT | ○ HERB | ○ FLOWER | ○ SHRUB | ○ TREE |
| ○ ANNUAL | ○ BIENNIAL | ○ PERENNIAL | ○ SEEDLING | | |

Care Instructions

Planting Instructions

Additional Notes

Fertilizer & Equipment

Fertilizer & Equipment

SIZE	☆☆☆☆☆
COLOR	☆☆☆☆☆
TASTE	☆☆☆☆☆

Name _____

Name

Location _____

GERMINATED	
PLANTED	
HARVESTED	

Supplier _____

Price _____

Started From

Light Level

○ SEED   ○ PLANT   ○ SUN   ○ PARTIAL SUN   ○ SHADE   ○ OTHER

Scientific Class

○ VEGETABLE   ○ FRUIT   ○ HERB   ○ FLOWER   ○ SHRUB   ○ TREE
○ ANNUAL   ○ BIENNIAL   ○ PERENNIAL   ○ SEEDLING

Care Instructions

Planting Instructions

Additional Notes

Fertilizer & Equipment

Fertilizer & Equipment

SIZE	☆☆☆☆☆
COLOR	☆☆☆☆☆
TASTE	☆☆☆☆☆

Name _____

Location _____

Supplier _____

Price _____

Name

GERMINATED	
PLANTED	
HARVESTED	

Started From

( ) SEED   ( ) PLANT

Light Level

( ) SUN   ( ) PARTIAL SUN   ( ) SHADE   ( ) OTHER

Scientific Class

( ) VEGETABLE   ( ) FRUIT   ( ) HERB   ( ) FLOWER   ( ) SHRUB   ( ) TREE

( ) ANNUAL   ( ) BIENNIAL   ( ) PERENNIAL   ( ) SEEDLING

Care Instructions

Planting Instructions

Additional Notes

Fertilizer & Equipment

Fertilizer & Equipment

SIZE	☆☆☆☆☆
COLOR	☆☆☆☆☆
TASTE	☆☆☆☆☆

Name _____

Location _____

Supplier _____

Price _____

Name

| GERMINATED |
| PLANTED |
| HARVESTED |

Started From

| ○ SEED | ○ PLANT |

Light Level

| ○ SUN | ○ PARTIAL SUN | ○ SHADE | ○ OTHER |

Scientific Class

| ○ VEGETABLE | ○ FRUIT | ○ HERB | ○ FLOWER | ○ SHRUB | ○ TREE |
| ○ ANNUAL | ○ BIENNIAL | ○ PERENNIAL | ○ SEEDLING | | |

Care Instructions

Planting Instructions

Additional Notes

Fertilizer & Equipment

Fertilizer & Equipment

SIZE	☆☆☆☆☆
COLOR	☆☆☆☆☆
TASTE	☆☆☆☆☆

Name _____

Location _____

Supplier _____

Price _____

Name

GERMINATED	
PLANTED	
HARVESTED	

Started From

- ○ SEED
- ○ PLANT

Light Level

- ○ SUN
- ○ PARTIAL SUN
- ○ SHADE
- ○ OTHER

Scientific Class

- ○ VEGETABLE
- ○ FRUIT
- ○ HERB
- ○ FLOWER
- ○ SHRUB
- ○ TREE
- ○ ANNUAL
- ○ BIENNIAL
- ○ PERENNIAL
- ○ SEEDLING

Care Instructions

Planting Instructions

Additional Notes

Fertilizer & Equipment

Fertilizer & Equipment

SIZE	☆☆☆☆☆
COLOR	☆☆☆☆☆
TASTE	☆☆☆☆☆

Name _____

Location _____

Supplier _____

Price _____

Name

GERMINATED	
PLANTED	
HARVESTED	

Started From

○ SEED   ○ PLANT

Light Level

○ SUN   ○ PARTIAL SUN   ○ SHADE   ○ OTHER

Scientific Class

○ VEGETABLE   ○ FRUIT   ○ HERB   ○ FLOWER   ○ SHRUB   ○ TREE
○ ANNUAL   ○ BIENNIAL   ○ PERENNIAL   ○ SEEDLING

Care Instructions

Planting Instructions

Additional Notes

Fertilizer & Equipment

Fertilizer & Equipment

SIZE	☆☆☆☆☆
COLOR	☆☆☆☆☆
TASTE	☆☆☆☆☆

Name _____

Location _____

Supplier _____

Price _____

Name

| GERMINATED |
| PLANTED |
| HARVESTED |

Started From

○ SEED ○ PLANT

Light Level

○ SUN ○ PARTIAL SUN ○ SHADE ○ OTHER

Scientific Class

○ VEGETABLE ○ FRUIT ○ HERB ○ FLOWER ○ SHRUB ○ TREE
○ ANNUAL ○ BIENNIAL ○ PERENNIAL ○ SEEDLING

Care Instructions

Planting Instructions

Additional Notes

Fertilizer & Equipment

Fertilizer & Equipment

SIZE	☆☆☆☆☆
COLOR	☆☆☆☆☆
TASTE	☆☆☆☆☆

Name _____

Location _____

Supplier _____

Price _____

Name

| GERMINATED |
| PLANTED |
| HARVESTED |

Started From

| ○ SEED | ○ PLANT | ○ SUN | ○ PARTIAL SUN | ○ SHADE | ○ OTHER |

Light Level

Scientific Class

| ○ VEGETABLE | ○ FRUIT | ○ HERB | ○ FLOWER | ○ SHRUB | ○ TREE |
| ○ ANNUAL | ○ BIENNIAL | ○ PERENNIAL | ○ SEEDLING | | |

Care Instructions

Planting Instructions

Additional Notes

Fertilizer & Equipment

Fertilizer & Equipment

SIZE	☆☆☆☆☆
COLOR	☆☆☆☆☆
TASTE	☆☆☆☆☆

Name _____

Location _____

Supplier _____

Price _____

Name

GERMINATED	
PLANTED	
HARVESTED	

Started From

○ SEED	○ PLANT

Light Level

○ SUN	○ PARTIAL SUN	○ SHADE	○ OTHER

Scientific Class

○ VEGETABLE	○ FRUIT	○ HERB	○ FLOWER	○ SHRUB	○ TREE
○ ANNUAL	○ BIENNIAL	○ PERENNIAL	○ SEEDLING		

Care Instructions

Planting Instructions

Additional Notes

Fertilizer & Equipment

Fertilizer & Equipment

SIZE	☆☆☆☆☆
COLOR	☆☆☆☆☆
TASTE	☆☆☆☆☆

Name _____

Location _____

Supplier _____

Price _____

Name

GERMINATED	
PLANTED	
HARVESTED	

Started From

○ SEED   ○ PLANT

Light Level

○ SUN   ○ PARTIAL SUN   ○ SHADE   ○ OTHER

Scientific Class

○ VEGETABLE   ○ FRUIT   ○ HERB   ○ FLOWER   ○ SHRUB   ○ TREE

○ ANNUAL   ○ BIENNIAL   ○ PERENNIAL   ○ SEEDLING

Care Instructions

Planting Instructions

Additional Notes

Fertilizer & Equipment

Fertilizer & Equipment

SIZE	☆☆☆☆☆
COLOR	☆☆☆☆☆
TASTE	☆☆☆☆☆

Name _____

Location _____

Supplier _____

Price _____

Name

| GERMINATED |
| PLANTED |
| HARVESTED |

Started From

( ) SEED   ( ) PLANT   ( ) SUN   ( ) PARTIAL SUN   ( ) SHADE   ( ) OTHER

Light Level

Scientific Class

( ) VEGETABLE   ( ) FRUIT   ( ) HERB   ( ) FLOWER   ( ) SHRUB   ( ) TREE
( ) ANNUAL   ( ) BIENNIAL   ( ) PERENNIAL   ( ) SEEDLING

Care Instructions

Planting Instructions

Additional Notes

Fertilizer & Equipment

Fertilizer & Equipment

SIZE	☆☆☆☆☆
COLOR	☆☆☆☆☆
TASTE	☆☆☆☆☆

Name _____

Location _____

Supplier _____

Price _____

Name

| GERMINATED |
| PLANTED |
| HARVESTED |

Started From

| ○ SEED | ○ PLANT |

Light Level

| ○ SUN | ○ PARTIAL SUN | ○ SHADE | ○ OTHER |

Scientific Class

| ○ VEGETABLE | ○ FRUIT | ○ HERB | ○ FLOWER | ○ SHRUB | ○ TREE |
| ○ ANNUAL | ○ BIENNIAL | ○ PERENNIAL | ○ SEEDLING |

Care Instructions

Planting Instructions

Additional Notes

Fertilizer & Equipment

Fertilizer & Equipment

SIZE	☆☆☆☆☆
COLOR	☆☆☆☆☆
TASTE	☆☆☆☆☆

Name _____

Location _____

Supplier _____

Price _____

Name

GERMINATED	
PLANTED	
HARVESTED	

Started From

○ SEED	○ PLANT

Light Level

○ SUN	○ PARTIAL SUN	○ SHADE	○ OTHER

Scientific Class

○ VEGETABLE	○ FRUIT	○ HERB	○ FLOWER	○ SHRUB	○ TREE
○ ANNUAL	○ BIENNIAL	○ PERENNIAL	○ SEEDLING		

Care Instructions

Planting Instructions

Additional Notes

Fertilizer & Equipment

Fertilizer & Equipment

SIZE	☆☆☆☆☆
COLOR	☆☆☆☆☆
TASTE	☆☆☆☆☆

Name _____

Name

GERMINATED	
PLANTED	
HARVESTED	

Location _____

Supplier _____

Price _____

Started From

○ SEED ○ PLANT ○ SUN ○ PARTIAL SUN ○ SHADE ○ OTHER

Light Level

Scientific Class

○ VEGETABLE ○ FRUIT ○ HERB ○ FLOWER ○ SHRUB ○ TREE
○ ANNUAL ○ BIENNIAL ○ PERENNIAL ○ SEEDLING

Care Instructions

Planting Instructions

Additional Notes

Fertilizer & Equipment

Fertilizer & Equipment

SIZE	☆☆☆☆☆
COLOR	☆☆☆☆☆
TASTE	☆☆☆☆☆

Name _____

Location _____

Supplier _____

Price _____

Name

| GERMINATED |
| PLANTED |
| HARVESTED |

Started From

○ SEED ○ PLANT

Light Level

○ SUN ○ PARTIAL SUN ○ SHADE ○ OTHER

Scientific Class

○ VEGETABLE ○ FRUIT ○ HERB ○ FLOWER ○ SHRUB ○ TREE
○ ANNUAL ○ BIENNIAL ○ PERENNIAL ○ SEEDLING

Care Instructions

Planting Instructions

Additional Notes

Fertilizer & Equipment

Fertilizer & Equipment

SIZE	☆☆☆☆☆
COLOR	☆☆☆☆☆
TASTE	☆☆☆☆☆

Name _____

Name

| GERMINATED |
| PLANTED |
| HARVESTED |

Location _____

Supplier _____

Price _____

Started From

| ○ SEED | ○ PLANT |

Light Level

| ○ SUN | ○ PARTIAL SUN | ○ SHADE | ○ OTHER |

Scientific Class

| ○ VEGETABLE | ○ FRUIT | ○ HERB | ○ FLOWER | ○ SHRUB | ○ TREE |
| ○ ANNUAL | ○ BIENNIAL | ○ PERENNIAL | ○ SEEDLING |

Care Instructions

Planting Instructions

Additional Notes

Fertilizer & Equipment

Fertilizer & Equipment

SIZE	☆☆☆☆☆
COLOR	☆☆☆☆☆
TASTE	☆☆☆☆☆

Name _____

Location _____

Supplier _____

Price _____

Name

GERMINATED	
PLANTED	
HARVESTED	

Started From

○ SEED	○ PLANT

Light Level

○ SUN	○ PARTIAL SUN	○ SHADE	○ OTHER

Scientific Class

○ VEGETABLE	○ FRUIT	○ HERB	○ FLOWER	○ SHRUB	○ TREE
○ ANNUAL	○ BIENNIAL	○ PERENNIAL	○ SEEDLING		

Care Instructions

Planting Instructions

Additional Notes

Fertilizer & Equipment

Fertilizer & Equipment

SIZE	☆☆☆☆☆
COLOR	☆☆☆☆☆
TASTE	☆☆☆☆☆

Name _____

Location _____

Supplier _____

Price _____

Name

GERMINATED	
PLANTED	
HARVESTED	

Started From

( ) SEED   ( ) PLANT

Light Level

( ) SUN   ( ) PARTIAL SUN   ( ) SHADE   ( ) OTHER

Scientific Class

( ) VEGETABLE   ( ) FRUIT   ( ) HERB   ( ) FLOWER   ( ) SHRUB   ( ) TREE
( ) ANNUAL   ( ) BIENNIAL   ( ) PERENNIAL   ( ) SEEDLING

Care Instructions

Planting Instructions

Additional Notes

Fertilizer & Equipment

Fertilizer & Equipment

SIZE	☆☆☆☆☆
COLOR	☆☆☆☆☆
TASTE	☆☆☆☆☆

Name _____

Location _____

Supplier _____

Price _____

Name

| GERMINATED |
| PLANTED |
| HARVESTED |

Started From

( ) SEED   ( ) PLANT

Light Level

( ) SUN   ( ) PARTIAL SUN   ( ) SHADE   ( ) OTHER

Scientific Class

( ) VEGETABLE   ( ) FRUIT   ( ) HERB   ( ) FLOWER   ( ) SHRUB   ( ) TREE

( ) ANNUAL   ( ) BIENNIAL   ( ) PERENNIAL   ( ) SEEDLING

Care Instructions

Planting Instructions

Additional Notes

Fertilizer & Equipment

Fertilizer & Equipment

SIZE	☆☆☆☆☆
COLOR	☆☆☆☆☆
TASTE	☆☆☆☆☆

Name _____

Name

Location _____

GERMINATED	
PLANTED	
HARVESTED	

Supplier _____

Price _____

Started From

Light Level

○ SEED   ○ PLANT   ○ SUN   ○ PARTIAL SUN   ○ SHADE   ○ OTHER

Scientific Class

○ VEGETABLE   ○ FRUIT   ○ HERB   ○ FLOWER   ○ SHRUB   ○ TREE
○ ANNUAL   ○ BIENNIAL   ○ PERENNIAL   ○ SEEDLING

Care Instructions

Planting Instructions

Additional Notes

Fertilizer & Equipment

Fertilizer & Equipment

SIZE	☆☆☆☆☆
COLOR	☆☆☆☆☆
TASTE	☆☆☆☆☆

Name _____

Location _____

Supplier _____

Price _____

Name

| GERMINATED |
| PLANTED |
| HARVESTED |

Started From

| SEED | PLANT | SUN | PARTIAL SUN | SHADE | OTHER |

Light Level

Scientific Class

| VEGETABLE | FRUIT | HERB | FLOWER | SHRUB | TREE |
| ANNUAL | BIENNIAL | PERENNIAL | SEEDLING | | |

Care Instructions

Planting Instructions

Additional Notes

Fertilizer & Equipment

Fertilizer & Equipment

SIZE	☆☆☆☆☆
COLOR	☆☆☆☆☆
TASTE	☆☆☆☆☆

Name _____

Location _____

Supplier _____

Price _____

Name

GERMINATED	
PLANTED	
HARVESTED	

Started From

Light Level

○ SEED   ○ PLANT   ○ SUN   ○ PARTIAL SUN   ○ SHADE   ○ OTHER

Scientific Class

○ VEGETABLE   ○ FRUIT   ○ HERB   ○ FLOWER   ○ SHRUB   ○ TREE
○ ANNUAL   ○ BIENNIAL   ○ PERENNIAL   ○ SEEDLING

Care Instructions

Planting Instructions

Additional Notes

Fertilizer & Equipment

Fertilizer & Equipment

SIZE	☆☆☆☆☆
COLOR	☆☆☆☆☆
TASTE	☆☆☆☆☆

Name _____

Location _____

Supplier _____

Price _____

Name

| GERMINATED |
| PLANTED |
| HARVESTED |

Started From

○ SEED   ○ PLANT

Light Level

○ SUN   ○ PARTIAL SUN   ○ SHADE   ○ OTHER

Scientific Class

○ VEGETABLE   ○ FRUIT   ○ HERB   ○ FLOWER   ○ SHRUB   ○ TREE
○ ANNUAL   ○ BIENNIAL   ○ PERENNIAL   ○ SEEDLING

Care Instructions

Planting Instructions

Additional Notes

Fertilizer & Equipment

Fertilizer & Equipment

SIZE	☆☆☆☆☆
COLOR	☆☆☆☆☆
TASTE	☆☆☆☆☆

Name _____

Name

GERMINATED	
PLANTED	
HARVESTED	

Location _____

Supplier _____

Price _____

Started From

( ) SEED   ( ) PLANT   ( ) SUN   ( ) PARTIAL SUN   ( ) SHADE   ( ) OTHER

Light Level

Scientific Class

( ) VEGETABLE   ( ) FRUIT   ( ) HERB   ( ) FLOWER   ( ) SHRUB   ( ) TREE
( ) ANNUAL   ( ) BIENNIAL   ( ) PERENNIAL   ( ) SEEDLING

Care Instructions

Planting Instructions

Additional Notes

Fertilizer & Equipment

Fertilizer & Equipment

SIZE	☆☆☆☆☆
COLOR	☆☆☆☆☆
TASTE	☆☆☆☆☆

Name _____

Location _____

Supplier _____

Price _____

Name

| GERMINATED |
| PLANTED |
| HARVESTED |

Started From

○ SEED   ○ PLANT

Light Level

○ SUN   ○ PARTIAL SUN   ○ SHADE   ○ OTHER

Scientific Class

○ VEGETABLE   ○ FRUIT   ○ HERB   ○ FLOWER   ○ SHRUB   ○ TREE
○ ANNUAL   ○ BIENNIAL   ○ PERENNIAL   ○ SEEDLING

Care Instructions

Planting Instructions

Additional Notes

Fertilizer & Equipment

Fertilizer & Equipment

SIZE	☆☆☆☆☆
COLOR	☆☆☆☆☆
TASTE	☆☆☆☆☆

Name _____

Location _____

Supplier _____

Price _____

Name

GERMINATED	
PLANTED	
HARVESTED	

Started From

○ SEED   ○ PLANT

Light Level

○ SUN   ○ PARTIAL SUN   ○ SHADE   ○ OTHER

Scientific Class

○ VEGETABLE   ○ FRUIT   ○ HERB   ○ FLOWER   ○ SHRUB   ○ TREE
○ ANNUAL   ○ BIENNIAL   ○ PERENNIAL   ○ SEEDLING

Care Instructions

Planting Instructions

Additional Notes

Fertilizer & Equipment

Fertilizer & Equipment

SIZE	☆☆☆☆☆
COLOR	☆☆☆☆☆
TASTE	☆☆☆☆☆

Name _____

Name

| GERMINATED |
| PLANTED |
| HARVESTED |

Location _____

Supplier _____

Price _____

Started From

| ○ SEED | ○ PLANT |

Light Level

| ○ SUN | ○ PARTIAL SUN | ○ SHADE | ○ OTHER |

Scientific Class

| ○ VEGETABLE | ○ FRUIT | ○ HERB | ○ FLOWER | ○ SHRUB | ○ TREE |
| ○ ANNUAL | ○ BIENNIAL | ○ PERENNIAL | ○ SEEDLING | | |

Care Instructions

Planting Instructions

Additional Notes

Fertilizer & Equipment

Fertilizer & Equipment

SIZE	☆☆☆☆☆
COLOR	☆☆☆☆☆
TASTE	☆☆☆☆☆

Name _____

Location _____

Supplier _____

Price _____

Name

| GERMINATED |
| PLANTED |
| HARVESTED |

Started From

( ) SEED   ( ) PLANT

Light Level

( ) SUN ( ) PARTIAL SUN ( ) SHADE ( ) OTHER

Scientific Class

( ) VEGETABLE ( ) FRUIT ( ) HERB ( ) FLOWER ( ) SHRUB ( ) TREE

( ) ANNUAL ( ) BIENNIAL ( ) PERENNIAL ( ) SEEDLING

Care Instructions

Planting Instructions

Additional Notes

Fertilizer & Equipment

Fertilizer & Equipment

SIZE	☆ ☆ ☆ ☆ ☆
COLOR	☆ ☆ ☆ ☆ ☆
TASTE	☆ ☆ ☆ ☆ ☆

Name _____

Location _____

Supplier _____

Price _____

Name

GERMINATED
PLANTED
HARVESTED

Started From

◯ SEED   ◯ PLANT

Light Level

◯ SUN   ◯ PARTIAL SUN   ◯ SHADE   ◯ OTHER

Scientific Class

◯ VEGETABLE   ◯ FRUIT   ◯ HERB   ◯ FLOWER   ◯ SHRUB   ◯ TREE

◯ ANNUAL   ◯ BIENNIAL   ◯ PERENNIAL   ◯ SEEDLING

Care Instructions

Planting Instructions

Additional Notes

Fertilizer & Equipment

Fertilizer & Equipment

SIZE	☆☆☆☆☆
COLOR	☆☆☆☆☆
TASTE	☆☆☆☆☆

Name _____

Location _____

Supplier _____

Price _____

Name

GERMINATED	
PLANTED	
HARVESTED	

Started From

◯ SEED   ◯ PLANT

Light Level

◯ SUN   ◯ PARTIAL SUN   ◯ SHADE   ◯ OTHER

Scientific Class

◯ VEGETABLE   ◯ FRUIT   ◯ HERB   ◯ FLOWER   ◯ SHRUB   ◯ TREE
◯ ANNUAL   ◯ BIENNIAL   ◯ PERENNIAL   ◯ SEEDLING

Care Instructions

Planting Instructions

Additional Notes

Fertilizer & Equipment

Fertilizer & Equipment

SIZE	☆☆☆☆☆
COLOR	☆☆☆☆☆
TASTE	☆☆☆☆☆

Name _____

Name

GERMINATED	
PLANTED	
HARVESTED	

Location _____

Supplier _____

Price _____

Started From

Light Level

○ SEED   ○ PLANT   ○ SUN   ○ PARTIAL SUN   ○ SHADE   ○ OTHER

Scientific Class

○ VEGETABLE   ○ FRUIT   ○ HERB   ○ FLOWER   ○ SHRUB   ○ TREE
○ ANNUAL   ○ BIENNIAL   ○ PERENNIAL   ○ SEEDLING

Care Instructions

Planting Instructions

Additional Notes

Fertilizer & Equipment

Fertilizer & Equipment

SIZE	☆☆☆☆☆
COLOR	☆☆☆☆☆
TASTE	☆☆☆☆☆

Name _____

Name

| GERMINATED |
| PLANTED |
| HARVESTED |

Location _____

Supplier _____

Price _____

Started From

Light Level

○ SEED   ○ PLANT   ○ SUN   ○ PARTIAL SUN   ○ SHADE   ○ OTHER

Scientific Class

○ VEGETABLE   ○ FRUIT   ○ HERB   ○ FLOWER   ○ SHRUB   ○ TREE
○ ANNUAL   ○ BIENNIAL   ○ PERENNIAL   ○ SEEDLING

Care Instructions

Planting Instructions

Additional Notes

Fertilizer & Equipment

Fertilizer & Equipment

SIZE	☆☆☆☆☆
COLOR	☆☆☆☆☆
TASTE	☆☆☆☆☆

Name _____

Location _____

Supplier _____

Price _____

Name

GERMINATED	
PLANTED	
HARVESTED	

Started From

Light Level

○ SEED	○ PLANT	○ SUN	○ PARTIAL SUN	○ SHADE	○ OTHER

Scientific Class

○ VEGETABLE	○ FRUIT	○ HERB	○ FLOWER	○ SHRUB	○ TREE
○ ANNUAL	○ BIENNIAL	○ PERENNIAL	○ SEEDLING		

Care Instructions

Planting Instructions

Additional Notes

Fertilizer & Equipment

Fertilizer & Equipment

SIZE	☆☆☆☆☆
COLOR	☆☆☆☆☆
TASTE	☆☆☆☆☆

Name _____

Location _____

Supplier _____

Price _____

Name

GERMINATED	
PLANTED	
HARVESTED	

Started From

○ SEED   ○ PLANT   ○ SUN   ○ PARTIAL SUN   ○ SHADE   ○ OTHER

Light Level

Scientific Class

○ VEGETABLE   ○ FRUIT   ○ HERB   ○ FLOWER   ○ SHRUB   ○ TREE
○ ANNUAL   ○ BIENNIAL ○ PERENNIAL ○ SEEDLING

Care Instructions

Planting Instructions

Additional Notes

Fertilizer & Equipment

Fertilizer & Equipment

SIZE	☆☆☆☆☆
COLOR	☆☆☆☆☆
TASTE	☆☆☆☆☆

Name _____

Location _____

Supplier _____

Price _____

Name

| GERMINATED |
| PLANTED |
| HARVESTED |

Started From

( ) SEED   ( ) PLANT   ( ) SUN   ( ) PARTIAL SUN   ( ) SHADE   ( ) OTHER

Light Level

Scientific Class

( ) VEGETABLE   ( ) FRUIT   ( ) HERB   ( ) FLOWER   ( ) SHRUB   ( ) TREE

( ) ANNUAL   ( ) BIENNIAL   ( ) PERENNIAL   ( ) SEEDLING

Care Instructions

Planting Instructions

Additional Notes

Fertilizer & Equipment

Fertilizer & Equipment

SIZE	☆☆☆☆☆
COLOR	☆☆☆☆☆
TASTE	☆☆☆☆☆

Name _____

Location _____

Supplier _____

Price _____

Name

GERMINATED	
PLANTED	
HARVESTED	

Started From

○ SEED   ○ PLANT

Light Level

○ SUN   ○ PARTIAL SUN   ○ SHADE   ○ OTHER

Scientific Class

○ VEGETABLE   ○ FRUIT   ○ HERB   ○ FLOWER   ○ SHRUB   ○ TREE
○ ANNUAL   ○ BIENNIAL   ○ PERENNIAL   ○ SEEDLING

Care Instructions

Planting Instructions

Additional Notes

Fertilizer & Equipment

Fertilizer & Equipment

SIZE	☆☆☆☆☆
COLOR	☆☆☆☆☆
TASTE	☆☆☆☆☆

Name _____

Location _____

Supplier _____

Price _____

Name

| GERMINATED |
| PLANTED |
| HARVESTED |

Started From

○ SEED ○ PLANT

Light Level

○ SUN ○ PARTIAL SUN ○ SHADE ○ OTHER

Scientific Class

○ VEGETABLE ○ FRUIT ○ HERB ○ FLOWER ○ SHRUB ○ TREE
○ ANNUAL ○ BIENNIAL ○ PERENNIAL ○ SEEDLING

Care Instructions

Planting Instructions

Additional Notes

Fertilizer & Equipment

Fertilizer & Equipment

SIZE	☆☆☆☆☆
COLOR	☆☆☆☆☆
TASTE	☆☆☆☆☆

Name _____

Location _____

Supplier _____

Price _____

Name

GERMINATED	
PLANTED	
HARVESTED	

Started From

○ SEED   ○ PLANT

Light Level

○ SUN   ○ PARTIAL SUN   ○ SHADE   ○ OTHER

Scientific Class

○ VEGETABLE   ○ FRUIT   ○ HERB   ○ FLOWER   ○ SHRUB   ○ TREE

○ ANNUAL   ○ BIENNIAL   ○ PERENNIAL   ○ SEEDLING

Care Instructions

Planting Instructions

Additional Notes

Fertilizer & Equipment

Fertilizer & Equipment

SIZE	☆☆☆☆☆
COLOR	☆☆☆☆☆
TASTE	☆☆☆☆☆

Name _____

Location _____

Supplier _____

Price _____

Name

GERMINATED	
PLANTED	
HARVESTED	

Started From

( ) SEED   ( ) PLANT

Light Level

( ) SUN   ( ) PARTIAL SUN   ( ) SHADE   ( ) OTHER

Scientific Class

( ) VEGETABLE   ( ) FRUIT   ( ) HERB   ( ) FLOWER   ( ) SHRUB   ( ) TREE

( ) ANNUAL   ( ) BIENNIAL   ( ) PERENNIAL   ( ) SEEDLING

Care Instructions

Planting Instructions

Additional Notes

Fertilizer & Equipment

Fertilizer & Equipment

SIZE	☆☆☆☆☆
COLOR	☆☆☆☆☆
TASTE	☆☆☆☆☆

Name _____

Location _____

Supplier _____

Price _____

Name

GERMINATED	
PLANTED	
HARVESTED	

Started From

( ) SEED   ( ) PLANT

Light Level

( ) SUN   ( ) PARTIAL SUN   ( ) SHADE   ( ) OTHER

Scientific Class

( ) VEGETABLE   ( ) FRUIT   ( ) HERB   ( ) FLOWER   ( ) SHRUB   ( ) TREE
( ) ANNUAL   ( ) BIENNIAL   ( ) PERENNIAL   ( ) SEEDLING

Care Instructions

Planting Instructions

Additional Notes

Fertilizer & Equipment

Fertilizer & Equipment

SIZE	☆☆☆☆☆
COLOR	☆☆☆☆☆
TASTE	☆☆☆☆☆

Name _____

Location _____

Supplier _____

Price _____

Name

| GERMINATED |
| PLANTED |
| HARVESTED |

Started From

○ SEED ○ PLANT

Light Level

○ SUN ○ PARTIAL SUN ○ SHADE ○ OTHER

Scientific Class

○ VEGETABLE ○ FRUIT ○ HERB ○ FLOWER ○ SHRUB ○ TREE
○ ANNUAL ○ BIENNIAL ○ PERENNIAL ○ SEEDLING

Care Instructions

Planting Instructions

Additional Notes

Fertilizer & Equipment

Fertilizer & Equipment

SIZE	☆☆☆☆☆
COLOR	☆☆☆☆☆
TASTE	☆☆☆☆☆

Name _____

Location _____

Supplier _____

Price _____

Name

GERMINATED	
PLANTED	
HARVESTED	

Started From

( ) SEED   ( ) PLANT

Light Level

( ) SUN   ( ) PARTIAL SUN   ( ) SHADE   ( ) OTHER

Scientific Class

( ) VEGETABLE   ( ) FRUIT   ( ) HERB   ( ) FLOWER   ( ) SHRUB   ( ) TREE

( ) ANNUAL   ( ) BIENNIAL   ( ) PERENNIAL   ( ) SEEDLING

Care Instructions

Planting Instructions

Additional Notes

Fertilizer & Equipment

Fertilizer & Equipment

SIZE	☆☆☆☆☆
COLOR	☆☆☆☆☆
TASTE	☆☆☆☆☆

Name _____

Location _____

Supplier _____

Price _____

Name

GERMINATED	
PLANTED	
HARVESTED	

Started From

○ SEED	○ PLANT

Light Level

○ SUN	○ PARTIAL SUN	○ SHADE	○ OTHER

Scientific Class

○ VEGETABLE	○ FRUIT	○ HERB	○ FLOWER	○ SHRUB	○ TREE
○ ANNUAL	○ BIENNIAL	○ PERENNIAL	○ SEEDLING		

Care Instructions

Planting Instructions

Additional Notes

Fertilizer & Equipment

Fertilizer & Equipment

SIZE	☆☆☆☆☆
COLOR	☆☆☆☆☆
TASTE	☆☆☆☆☆

Name _____

Location _____

Supplier _____

Price _____

Name

GERMINATED	
PLANTED	
HARVESTED	

Started From

○ SEED   ○ PLANT

Light Level

○ SUN   ○ PARTIAL SUN   ○ SHADE   ○ OTHER

Scientific Class

○ VEGETABLE   ○ FRUIT   ○ HERB   ○ FLOWER   ○ SHRUB   ○ TREE
○ ANNUAL   ○ BIENNIAL   ○ PERENNIAL   ○ SEEDLING

Care Instructions

Planting Instructions

Additional Notes

Fertilizer & Equipment

Fertilizer & Equipment

SIZE	☆☆☆☆☆
COLOR	☆☆☆☆☆
TASTE	☆☆☆☆☆

Name _____

Location _____

Supplier _____

Price _____

Name

| GERMINATED |
| PLANTED |
| HARVESTED |

Started From

| ○ SEED | ○ PLANT |

Light Level

| ○ SUN | ○ PARTIAL SUN | ○ SHADE | ○ OTHER |

Scientific Class

| ○ VEGETABLE | ○ FRUIT | ○ HERB | ○ FLOWER | ○ SHRUB | ○ TREE |
| ○ ANNUAL | ○ BIENNIAL | ○ PERENNIAL | ○ SEEDLING | | |

Care Instructions

Planting Instructions

Additional Notes

Fertilizer & Equipment

Fertilizer & Equipment

SIZE	☆☆☆☆☆
COLOR	☆☆☆☆☆
TASTE	☆☆☆☆☆

Name _____

Name

| GERMINATED |
| PLANTED |
| HARVESTED |

Started From

○ SEED   ○ PLANT

Location _____

Supplier _____

Price _____

Light Level

○ SUN   ○ PARTIAL SUN   ○ SHADE   ○ OTHER

Scientific Class

○ VEGETABLE   ○ FRUIT   ○ HERB   ○ FLOWER   ○ SHRUB   ○ TREE
○ ANNUAL   ○ BIENNIAL   ○ PERENNIAL   ○ SEEDLING

Care Instructions

Planting Instructions

Additional Notes

Fertilizer & Equipment

Fertilizer & Equipment

SIZE	☆☆☆☆☆
COLOR	☆☆☆☆☆
TASTE	☆☆☆☆☆

Name _____

Location _____

Supplier _____

Price _____

Name

| GERMINATED |
| PLANTED |
| HARVESTED |

Started From

( ) SEED   ( ) PLANT   ( ) SUN

Light Level

( ) PARTIAL SUN   ( ) SHADE   ( ) OTHER

Scientific Class

( ) VEGETABLE   ( ) FRUIT   ( ) HERB   ( ) FLOWER   ( ) SHRUB   ( ) TREE

( ) ANNUAL   ( ) BIENNIAL   ( ) PERENNIAL   ( ) SEEDLING

Care Instructions

Planting Instructions

Additional Notes

Fertilizer & Equipment

Fertilizer & Equipment

SIZE	☆☆☆☆☆
COLOR	☆☆☆☆☆
TASTE	☆☆☆☆☆

Name _____

Location _____

Supplier _____

Price _____

Name

GERMINATED
PLANTED
HARVESTED

Started From

- ( ) SEED
- ( ) PLANT

Light Level

- ( ) SUN
- ( ) PARTIAL SUN
- ( ) SHADE
- ( ) OTHER

Scientific Class

- ( ) VEGETABLE
- ( ) FRUIT
- ( ) HERB
- ( ) FLOWER
- ( ) SHRUB
- ( ) TREE
- ( ) ANNUAL
- ( ) BIENNIAL
- ( ) PERENNIAL
- ( ) SEEDLING

Care Instructions

Planting Instructions

Additional Notes

Fertilizer & Equipment

Fertilizer & Equipment

SIZE	☆☆☆☆☆
COLOR	☆☆☆☆☆
TASTE	☆☆☆☆☆

Name _____

Location _____

Supplier _____

Price _____

Name

| GERMINATED |
| PLANTED |
| HARVESTED |

Started From

( ) SEED   ( ) PLANT

Light Level

( ) SUN   ( ) PARTIAL SUN   ( ) SHADE   ( ) OTHER

Scientific Class

( ) VEGETABLE   ( ) FRUIT   ( ) HERB   ( ) FLOWER   ( ) SHRUB   ( ) TREE
( ) ANNUAL   ( ) BIENNIAL   ( ) PERENNIAL   ( ) SEEDLING

Care Instructions

Planting Instructions

Additional Notes

Fertilizer & Equipment

Fertilizer & Equipment

SIZE	☆☆☆☆☆
COLOR	☆☆☆☆☆
TASTE	☆☆☆☆☆

Name _____

Location _____

Supplier _____

Price _____

Name

GERMINATED
PLANTED
HARVESTED

Started From

○ SEED   ○ PLANT

Light Level

○ SUN   ○ PARTIAL SUN   ○ SHADE   ○ OTHER

Scientific Class

○ VEGETABLE   ○ FRUIT   ○ HERB   ○ FLOWER   ○ SHRUB   ○ TREE

○ ANNUAL   ○ BIENNIAL   ○ PERENNIAL   ○ SEEDLING

Care Instructions

Planting Instructions

Additional Notes

Fertilizer & Equipment

Fertilizer & Equipment

SIZE	☆☆☆☆☆
COLOR	☆☆☆☆☆
TASTE	☆☆☆☆☆

Name _____

Location _____

Supplier _____

Price _____

Name

GERMINATED	
PLANTED	
HARVESTED	

Started From

○ SEED ○ PLANT

Light Level

○ SUN ○ PARTIAL SUN ○ SHADE ○ OTHER

Scientific Class

○ VEGETABLE ○ FRUIT ○ HERB ○ FLOWER ○ SHRUB ○ TREE

○ ANNUAL ○ BIENNIAL ○ PERENNIAL ○ SEEDLING

Care Instructions

Planting Instructions

Additional Notes

Fertilizer & Equipment

Fertilizer & Equipment

SIZE	☆☆☆☆☆
COLOR	☆☆☆☆☆
TASTE	☆☆☆☆☆

Name _____

Location _____

Supplier _____

Price _____

Name

GERMINATED	
PLANTED	
HARVESTED	

Started From

○ SEED   ○ PLANT

Light Level

○ SUN   ○ PARTIAL SUN   ○ SHADE   ○ OTHER

Scientific Class

○ VEGETABLE   ○ FRUIT   ○ HERB   ○ FLOWER   ○ SHRUB   ○ TREE
○ ANNUAL   ○ BIENNIAL   ○ PERENNIAL   ○ SEEDLING

Care Instructions

Planting Instructions

Additional Notes

Fertilizer & Equipment

Fertilizer & Equipment

SIZE	☆☆☆☆☆
COLOR	☆☆☆☆☆
TASTE	☆☆☆☆☆

Name _____

Location _____

Supplier _____

Price _____

Name

GERMINATED	
PLANTED	
HARVESTED	

Started From

( ) SEED   ( ) PLANT

Light Level

( ) SUN   ( ) PARTIAL SUN   ( ) SHADE   ( ) OTHER

Scientific Class

( ) VEGETABLE   ( ) FRUIT   ( ) HERB   ( ) FLOWER   ( ) SHRUB   ( ) TREE

( ) ANNUAL   ( ) BIENNIAL   ( ) PERENNIAL   ( ) SEEDLING

Care Instructions

Planting Instructions

Additional Notes

Fertilizer & Equipment

Fertilizer & Equipment

SIZE	☆☆☆☆☆
COLOR	☆☆☆☆☆
TASTE	☆☆☆☆☆

Name _____

Location _____

Supplier _____

Price _____

Name

| GERMINATED |
| PLANTED |
| HARVESTED |

Started From

◯ SEED   ◯ PLANT

Light Level

◯ SUN   ◯ PARTIAL SUN   ◯ SHADE   ◯ OTHER

Scientific Class

◯ VEGETABLE   ◯ FRUIT   ◯ HERB   ◯ FLOWER   ◯ SHRUB   ◯ TREE
◯ ANNUAL   ◯ BIENNIAL   ◯ PERENNIAL   ◯ SEEDLING

Care Instructions

Planting Instructions

Additional Notes

Fertilizer & Equipment

Fertilizer & Equipment

SIZE	☆☆☆☆☆
COLOR	☆☆☆☆☆
TASTE	☆☆☆☆☆

Name _____

Name

Location _____

Supplier _____

Price _____

GERMINATED	
PLANTED	
HARVESTED	

Started From

○ SEED　　○ PLANT　　○ SUN　　○ PARTIAL SUN　　○ SHADE　　○ OTHER

Light Level

Scientific Class

○ VEGETABLE　　○ FRUIT　　○ HERB　　○ FLOWER　　○ SHRUB　　○ TREE

○ ANNUAL　　○ BIENNIAL　　○ PERENNIAL　　○ SEEDLING

Care Instructions

Planting Instructions

Additional Notes

Fertilizer & Equipment

Fertilizer & Equipment

SIZE	☆☆☆☆☆
COLOR	☆☆☆☆☆
TASTE	☆☆☆☆☆

Name _____

Location _____

Supplier _____

Price _____

Name

GERMINATED	
PLANTED	
HARVESTED	

Started From

- ( ) SEED
- ( ) PLANT

Light Level

- ( ) SUN
- ( ) PARTIAL SUN
- ( ) SHADE
- ( ) OTHER

Scientific Class

- ( ) VEGETABLE
- ( ) FRUIT
- ( ) HERB
- ( ) FLOWER
- ( ) SHRUB
- ( ) TREE
- ( ) ANNUAL
- ( ) BIENNIAL
- ( ) PERENNIAL
- ( ) SEEDLING

Care Instructions

Planting Instructions

Additional Notes

Fertilizer & Equipment

Fertilizer & Equipment

SIZE	☆☆☆☆☆
COLOR	☆☆☆☆☆
TASTE	☆☆☆☆☆

Name _____

Location _____

Supplier _____

Price _____

Name

| GERMINATED |
| PLANTED |
| HARVESTED |

Started From

( ) SEED   ( ) PLANT   ( ) SUN   ( ) PARTIAL SUN   ( ) SHADE   ( ) OTHER

Light Level

Scientific Class

( ) VEGETABLE   ( ) FRUIT   ( ) HERB   ( ) FLOWER   ( ) SHRUB   ( ) TREE
( ) ANNUAL   ( ) BIENNIAL   ( ) PERENNIAL   ( ) SEEDLING

Care Instructions

Planting Instructions

Additional Notes

Fertilizer & Equipment

Fertilizer & Equipment

SIZE	☆☆☆☆☆
COLOR	☆☆☆☆☆
TASTE	☆☆☆☆☆

Name _____

Location _____

Supplier _____

Price _____

Name

GERMINATED	
PLANTED	
HARVESTED	

Started From

○ SEED   ○ PLANT

Light Level

○ SUN   ○ PARTIAL SUN   ○ SHADE   ○ OTHER

Scientific Class

○ VEGETABLE   ○ FRUIT   ○ HERB   ○ FLOWER   ○ SHRUB   ○ TREE
○ ANNUAL   ○ BIENNIAL   ○ PERENNIAL   ○ SEEDLING

Care Instructions

Planting Instructions

Additional Notes

Fertilizer & Equipment

Fertilizer & Equipment

SIZE	☆☆☆☆☆
COLOR	☆☆☆☆☆
TASTE	☆☆☆☆☆

Name _____

Location _____

Supplier _____

Price _____

Name

GERMINATED	
PLANTED	
HARVESTED	

Started From

○ SEED   ○ PLANT   ○ SUN

Light Level

○ PARTIAL SUN   ○ SHADE   ○ OTHER

Scientific Class

○ VEGETABLE   ○ FRUIT   ○ HERB   ○ FLOWER   ○ SHRUB   ○ TREE

○ ANNUAL   ○ BIENNIAL   ○ PERENNIAL   ○ SEEDLING

Care Instructions

Planting Instructions

Additional Notes

Fertilizer & Equipment

Fertilizer & Equipment

SIZE	☆☆☆☆☆
COLOR	☆☆☆☆☆
TASTE	☆☆☆☆☆

Name _____

Location _____

Supplier _____

Price _____

Name

GERMINATED
PLANTED
HARVESTED

Started From

○ SEED   ○ PLANT

Light Level

○ SUN   ○ PARTIAL SUN   ○ SHADE   ○ OTHER

Scientific Class

○ VEGETABLE   ○ FRUIT   ○ HERB   ○ FLOWER   ○ SHRUB   ○ TREE
○ ANNUAL   ○ BIENNIAL   ○ PERENNIAL   ○ SEEDLING

Care Instructions

Planting Instructions

Additional Notes

Fertilizer & Equipment

Fertilizer & Equipment

SIZE	☆☆☆☆☆
COLOR	☆☆☆☆☆
TASTE	☆☆☆☆☆

Name _____

Location _____

Supplier _____

Price _____

Name

GERMINATED
PLANTED
HARVESTED

Started From

○ SEED ○ PLANT ○ SUN ○ PARTIAL SUN ○ SHADE ○ OTHER

Light Level

Scientific Class

○ VEGETABLE ○ FRUIT ○ HERB ○ FLOWER ○ SHRUB ○ TREE
○ ANNUAL ○ BIENNIAL ○ PERENNIAL ○ SEEDLING

Care Instructions

Planting Instructions

Additional Notes

Fertilizer & Equipment

Fertilizer & Equipment

SIZE	☆☆☆☆☆
COLOR	☆☆☆☆☆
TASTE	☆☆☆☆☆

Name _____

Location _____

Supplier _____

Price _____

Name

GERMINATED	
PLANTED	
HARVESTED	

Started From

○ SEED   ○ PLANT

Light Level

○ SUN   ○ PARTIAL SUN   ○ SHADE   ○ OTHER

Scientific Class

○ VEGETABLE   ○ FRUIT   ○ HERB   ○ FLOWER   ○ SHRUB   ○ TREE

○ ANNUAL   ○ BIENNIAL   ○ PERENNIAL   ○ SEEDLING

Care Instructions

Planting Instructions

Additional Notes

Fertilizer & Equipment

Fertilizer & Equipment

SIZE	☆☆☆☆☆
COLOR	☆☆☆☆☆
TASTE	☆☆☆☆☆

Name _____

Location _____

Supplier _____

Price _____

Name

GERMINATED	
PLANTED	
HARVESTED	

Started From

( ) SEED   ( ) PLANT

Light Level

( ) SUN   ( ) PARTIAL SUN   ( ) SHADE   ( ) OTHER

Scientific Class

( ) VEGETABLE   ( ) FRUIT   ( ) HERB   ( ) FLOWER   ( ) SHRUB   ( ) TREE

( ) ANNUAL   ( ) BIENNIAL   ( ) PERENNIAL   ( ) SEEDLING

Care Instructions

Planting Instructions

Additional Notes

Fertilizer & Equipment

Fertilizer & Equipment

SIZE	☆☆☆☆☆
COLOR	☆☆☆☆☆
TASTE	☆☆☆☆☆

Name _____

Location _____

Supplier _____

Price _____

Name

GERMINATED	
PLANTED	
HARVESTED	

Started From

○ SEED   ○ PLANT

Light Level

○ SUN   ○ PARTIAL SUN   ○ SHADE   ○ OTHER

Scientific Class

○ VEGETABLE   ○ FRUIT   ○ HERB   ○ FLOWER   ○ SHRUB   ○ TREE
○ ANNUAL   ○ BIENNIAL   ○ PERENNIAL   ○ SEEDLING

Care Instructions

Planting Instructions

Additional Notes

Fertilizer & Equipment

Fertilizer & Equipment

SIZE	☆☆☆☆☆
COLOR	☆☆☆☆☆
TASTE	☆☆☆☆☆

Name _____

Location _____

Supplier _____

Price _____

Name

| GERMINATED |
| PLANTED |
| HARVESTED |

Started From

◯ SEED   ◯ PLANT

Light Level

◯ SUN   ◯ PARTIAL SUN   ◯ SHADE   ◯ OTHER

Scientific Class

◯ VEGETABLE   ◯ FRUIT   ◯ HERB   ◯ FLOWER   ◯ SHRUB   ◯ TREE
◯ ANNUAL   ◯ BIENNIAL   ◯ PERENNIAL   ◯ SEEDLING

Care Instructions

Planting Instructions

Additional Notes

Fertilizer & Equipment

Fertilizer & Equipment

SIZE	☆☆☆☆☆
COLOR	☆☆☆☆☆
TASTE	☆☆☆☆☆

Name _____

Location _____

Supplier _____

Price _____

Name

GERMINATED	
PLANTED	
HARVESTED	

Started From

○ SEED　　○ PLANT

Light Level

○ SUN　　○ PARTIAL SUN　　○ SHADE　　○ OTHER

Scientific Class

○ VEGETABLE　　○ FRUIT　　○ HERB　　○ FLOWER　　○ SHRUB　　○ TREE

○ ANNUAL　　○ BIENNIAL　　○ PERENNIAL　　○ SEEDLING

Care Instructions

Planting Instructions

Additional Notes

Fertilizer & Equipment

Fertilizer & Equipment

SIZE	☆☆☆☆☆
COLOR	☆☆☆☆☆
TASTE	☆☆☆☆☆

Name _____

Location _____

Supplier _____

Price _____

Name

GERMINATED	
PLANTED	
HARVESTED	

Started From

◯ SEED ◯ PLANT

Light Level

◯ SUN ◯ PARTIAL SUN ◯ SHADE ◯ OTHER

Scientific Class

◯ VEGETABLE ◯ FRUIT ◯ HERB ◯ FLOWER ◯ SHRUB ◯ TREE

◯ ANNUAL ◯ BIENNIAL ◯ PERENNIAL ◯ SEEDLING

Care Instructions

Planting Instructions

Additional Notes

Fertilizer & Equipment

Fertilizer & Equipment

SIZE	☆☆☆☆☆
COLOR	☆☆☆☆☆
TASTE	☆☆☆☆☆

Name _____

Location _____

Supplier _____

Price _____

Name

GERMINATED	
PLANTED	
HARVESTED	

Started From

( ) SEED   ( ) PLANT

Light Level

( ) SUN   ( ) PARTIAL SUN   ( ) SHADE   ( ) OTHER

Scientific Class

( ) VEGETABLE   ( ) FRUIT   ( ) HERB   ( ) FLOWER   ( ) SHRUB   ( ) TREE

( ) ANNUAL   ( ) BIENNIAL   ( ) PERENNIAL   ( ) SEEDLING

Care Instructions

Planting Instructions

Additional Notes

Fertilizer & Equipment

Fertilizer & Equipment

SIZE	☆☆☆☆☆
COLOR	☆☆☆☆☆
TASTE	☆☆☆☆☆

Name _____

Location _____

Supplier _____

Price _____

Name

GERMINATED	
PLANTED	
HARVESTED	

Started From

( ) SEED   ( ) PLANT

Light Level

( ) SUN   ( ) PARTIAL SUN   ( ) SHADE   ( ) OTHER

Scientific Class

( ) VEGETABLE   ( ) FRUIT   ( ) HERB   ( ) FLOWER   ( ) SHRUB   ( ) TREE

( ) ANNUAL   ( ) BIENNIAL   ( ) PERENNIAL   ( ) SEEDLING

Care Instructions

Planting Instructions

Additional Notes

Fertilizer & Equipment

Fertilizer & Equipment

SIZE	☆☆☆☆☆
COLOR	☆☆☆☆☆
TASTE	☆☆☆☆☆

Name _____

Location _____

Supplier _____

Price _____

Name

GERMINATED	
PLANTED	
HARVESTED	

Started From

○ SEED   ○ PLANT

Light Level

○ SUN   ○ PARTIAL SUN   ○ SHADE   ○ OTHER

Scientific Class

○ VEGETABLE   ○ FRUIT   ○ HERB   ○ FLOWER   ○ SHRUB   ○ TREE
○ ANNUAL   ○ BIENNIAL   ○ PERENNIAL   ○ SEEDLING

Care Instructions

Planting Instructions

Additional Notes

Fertilizer & Equipment

Fertilizer & Equipment

SIZE	☆☆☆☆☆
COLOR	☆☆☆☆☆
TASTE	☆☆☆☆☆

Name _____

Location _____

Supplier _____

Price _____

Name

GERMINATED	
PLANTED	
HARVESTED	

Started From

Light Level

○ SEED　　○ PLANT　　○ SUN　○ PARTIAL SUN　　○ SHADE　○ OTHER

Scientific Class

○ VEGETABLE　○ FRUIT　○ HERB　○ FLOWER　○ SHRUB　○ TREE
○ ANNUAL　○ BIENNIAL　○ PERENNIAL　○ SEEDLING

Care Instructions

Planting Instructions

Additional Notes

Fertilizer & Equipment

Fertilizer & Equipment

SIZE	☆☆☆☆☆
COLOR	☆☆☆☆☆
TASTE	☆☆☆☆☆

Name _____

Location _____

Supplier _____

Price _____

Name

| GERMINATED |
| PLANTED |
| HARVESTED |

Started From

( ) SEED ( ) PLANT

Light Level

( ) SUN ( ) PARTIAL SUN ( ) SHADE ( ) OTHER

Scientific Class

( ) VEGETABLE ( ) FRUIT ( ) HERB ( ) FLOWER ( ) SHRUB ( ) TREE
( ) ANNUAL ( ) BIENNIAL ( ) PERENNIAL ( ) SEEDLING

Care Instructions

Planting Instructions

Additional Notes

Fertilizer & Equipment

Fertilizer & Equipment

SIZE	☆☆☆☆☆
COLOR	☆☆☆☆☆
TASTE	☆☆☆☆☆

Name _____

Location _____

Supplier _____

Price _____

Name

GERMINATED	
PLANTED	
HARVESTED	

Started From

○ SEED	○ PLANT	○ SUN

Light Level

○ PARTIAL SUN	○ SHADE	○ OTHER

Scientific Class

○ VEGETABLE	○ FRUIT	○ HERB	○ FLOWER	○ SHRUB	○ TREE
○ ANNUAL	○ BIENNIAL	○ PERENNIAL	○ SEEDLING		

Care Instructions

Planting Instructions

Additional Notes

Fertilizer & Equipment

Fertilizer & Equipment

SIZE	☆☆☆☆☆
COLOR	☆☆☆☆☆
TASTE	☆☆☆☆☆

Name _____

Location _____

Supplier _____

Price _____

Name

| GERMINATED |
| PLANTED |
| HARVESTED |

Started From

○ SEED   ○ PLANT

Light Level

○ SUN   ○ PARTIAL SUN   ○ SHADE   ○ OTHER

Scientific Class

○ VEGETABLE   ○ FRUIT   ○ HERB   ○ FLOWER   ○ SHRUB   ○ TREE

○ ANNUAL   ○ BIENNIAL   ○ PERENNIAL   ○ SEEDLING

Care Instructions

Planting Instructions

Additional Notes

Fertilizer & Equipment

Fertilizer & Equipment

SIZE	☆☆☆☆☆
COLOR	☆☆☆☆☆
TASTE	☆☆☆☆☆

Name _____

Location _____

Supplier _____

Price _____

Name

GERMINATED	
PLANTED	
HARVESTED	

Started From

( ) SEED   ( ) PLANT   ( ) SUN   ( ) PARTIAL SUN   ( ) SHADE   ( ) OTHER

Light Level

Scientific Class

( ) VEGETABLE   ( ) FRUIT   ( ) HERB   ( ) FLOWER   ( ) SHRUB   ( ) TREE

( ) ANNUAL   ( ) BIENNIAL   ( ) PERENNIAL   ( ) SEEDLING

Care Instructions

Planting Instructions

Additional Notes

Fertilizer & Equipment

Fertilizer & Equipment

SIZE	☆☆☆☆☆
COLOR	☆☆☆☆☆
TASTE	☆☆☆☆☆

Name _____

Location _____

Supplier _____

Price _____

Name

GERMINATED	
PLANTED	
HARVESTED	

Started From

○ SEED   ○ PLANT

Light Level

○ SUN   ○ PARTIAL SUN   ○ SHADE   ○ OTHER

Scientific Class

○ VEGETABLE   ○ FRUIT   ○ HERB   ○ FLOWER   ○ SHRUB   ○ TREE

○ ANNUAL   ○ BIENNIAL   ○ PERENNIAL   ○ SEEDLING

Care Instructions

Planting Instructions

Additional Notes

Fertilizer & Equipment

Fertilizer & Equipment

SIZE	☆☆☆☆☆
COLOR	☆☆☆☆☆
TASTE	☆☆☆☆☆

Name _____

Location _____

Supplier _____

Price _____

Name

GERMINATED	
PLANTED	
HARVESTED	

Started From

Light Level

◯ SEED   ◯ PLANT   ◯ SUN   ◯ PARTIAL SUN   ◯ SHADE   ◯ OTHER

Scientific Class

◯ VEGETABLE   ◯ FRUIT   ◯ HERB   ◯ FLOWER   ◯ SHRUB   ◯ TREE
◯ ANNUAL   ◯ BIENNIAL   ◯ PERENNIAL   ◯ SEEDLING

Care Instructions

Planting Instructions

Additional Notes

Fertilizer & Equipment

Fertilizer & Equipment

SIZE	☆☆☆☆☆
COLOR	☆☆☆☆☆
TASTE	☆☆☆☆☆

2023

January

SUN	MON	TUE	WED	THU	FRI	SAT
1	2	3	4	5	6	7
8	9	10	11	12	13	14
15	16	17	18	19	20	21
22	23	24	25	26	27	28
29	30	31				

February

SUN	MON	TUE	WED	THU	FRI	SAT
			1	2	3	4
5	6	7	8	9	10	11
12	13	14	15	16	17	18
19	20	21	22	23	24	25
26	27	28				

March

SUN	MON	TUE	WED	THU	FRI	SAT
			1	2	3	4
5	6	7	8	9	10	11
12	13	14	15	16	17	18
19	20	21	22	23	24	25
26	27	28	29	30	31	

April

SUN	MON	TUE	WED	THU	FRI	SAT
						1
2	3	4	5	6	7	8
9	10	11	12	13	14	15
16	17	1t8	19	20	21	22
23	24	25	26	27	28	29
30						

May

SUN	MON	TUE	WED	THU	FRI	SAT
	1	2	3	4	5	6
7	8	9	10	11	12	13
14	15	16	17	18	19	20
21	22	23	24	25	26	27
28	29	30	31			

June

SUN	MON	TUE	WED	THU	FRI	SAT
				1	2	3
4	5	6	7	8	9	10
11	12	13	14	15	16	17
18	19	20	21	22	23	24
25	26	27	28	29	30	

July

SUN	MON	TUE	WED	THU	FRI	SAT
						1
2	3	4	5	6	7	8
9	10	11	12	13	14	15
16	17	18	19	20	21	22
23	24	25	26	27	28	29
30	31					

August

SUN	MON	TUE	WED	THU	FRI	SAT
		1	2	3	4	5
6	7	8	9	10	11	12
13	14	15	16	17	18	19
20	21	22	23	24	25	26
27	28	29	30	31		

September

SUN	MON	TUE	WED	THU	FRI	SAT
					1	2
3	4	5	6	7	8	9
10	11	12	13	14	15	16
17	18	19	20	21	22	23
24	25	26	27	28	29	30

October

SUN	MON	TUE	WED	THU	FRI	SAT
1	2	3	4	5	6	
7	8	9	10	11	12	13
14	15	16	17	18	19	20
21	22	23	24	25	26	27
28	29	30	31			

November

SUN	MON	TUE	WED	THU	FRI	SAT
			1	2	3	
4	5	6	7	8	9	10
11	12	13	14	15	16	17
18	19	20	21	22	23	24
25	26	27	28	29	30	

December

SUN	MON	TUE	WED	THU	FRI	SAT
						1
2	3	4	5	6	7	8
9	10	11	12	13	14	15
16	17	18	19	20	21	22
23	24	25	26	27	28	29
30	31					

Printed in Great Britain
by Amazon

23657533R10057